Eileen Duncan — with all good wishes
Val Warner
2 · v · 81

4

UNDER THE PENTHOUSE

Val Warner's poems have been praised for their truth to varied and sometimes painful experience. Her forms are modern and sure, her language
works with precision to bring complex images and incidents alive.

Born in 1946, she read history at Oxford and has worked as a librarian and
teacher. Her first collection of poems, *These Yellow Photos*, appeared as a
Carcanet booklet in 1971. She has translated a selection of the poems of
Tristan Corbière (*Wrecks*, 1973) for Carcanet.

UNDER
THE
PENTHOUSE
Val Warner

A CARCANET PRESS PUBLICATION

Acknowledgements and thanks are due to the editors of the following magazines, in which some of these poems have previously appeared: *Ambit, The Dublin Magazine, Ostrich, Poetry Review, Tribune* and *Workshop.*

SBN 902145 87 8 – cloth
SBN 902145 88 6 – paper

First published 1973
by Carcanet Press Ltd
266 Councillor Lane
Cheadle Hulme, Cheadle
Cheshire

Printed in Great Britain by
W & J Mackay Limited
Chatham

CONTENTS

'a few old images always the same no more blue the blue is done never was
the sack the arms the body the mud the dark living hair and nails all that'

Samuel Beckett *How It Is* (Calder & Boyars)

TOTTER

In morning twilight a dumpy figure hurrying to work
Down the mews, not very down at heel
Middle-aged, a black shopping bag
Held across her like a shield.
She sorts through a psychedelic carrier bag
Leant against a dustbin with a moss-green Harrods' one.
Rosé rinses the stucco fronts
Icing on the sky's high altar.
Too early for the milkman, though
Only powder for her.
Few letters, the odd bill. In luck today though,
From the newest dustbin she plucks
A pair of man's shoes, another shopping bag
She stuffs into hers. Dowdy magpie,
Through faint mist darting now from bin to bin
Slower nothing else today except a big black polythene bag
Statuesque with refuse, she empties into a bin
Potato peelings and chips of bronze chrysanthemum petals
Running down the side, and stuffs it dripping into hers.
Most of the residents are still asleep.

COLLAPSIBLE SECRETARY

At first work was quite separate;
She took the past to bed,
With teddy eyeless from a previous fray
Lording it on the counterpane all day,
A mascot from the more affluent past,
In the spick flat shared with two girl-friends.

A sea change came to the finely accoutred bird
Who first attracted. Things went.
The same clothes all week, shoes down at heel.
Nothing replaced. The transistor played
'I'm gonna wash that man right out of my hair.'
Her hair looked like it wanted washing.

On the tube, the news went home more
Glimpsed between the backs of business men
Shots and a variety of killing trembled
Something as her station swam up.
Work a strain, unemployment also became
For real, despite her racy speeds.

Her handbag clicks on an ancient letter
Wearing out, like the old prescription:
The bottom half of a perfume stick
Started where her otherwise neat future
Was blinded. Compact, and the front door key
Of the friend she made yesterday.

T.V. AERIALS

Another skyline another town the rain
It raineth in my heart
On the plain the *embarras de richesses*
Of young memory, a line of shaky aerials
Breezing across their sky seemed romantic
He'd latched on to their jagged fence
Where dawn hung bloody washing
Something else to remember by, that tide on the turn:
Now the barbed wire fence round a compound, looking in or out.
Or sinuously into waving fronds
Suggested death by water, the letters danced
A child learning to read
The writing on the wall inside his head
Between the press of business appointments, their ring tightened
Their grip on him. Crazy dolmens
Strung across his window, so many distorted arms outstretched
For amusement. A fence against
Nothing. His life blood now, he worked in the media.
And had his nightmares, twisted
Crucifixes, cabalistic £ s d signs
Barbed wire the clouds just escaped
Being torn apart on he missed the electric fence
Keeping the animals all safely in.

Somebody else would have to pay the gas bill.
Non-events have concussed her head.
Easy as a penny in the slot,
Just the bolt drawn back
And the door left banging in the gale
In the dark night of the lone
Interest in herself
Knowledge the ulcer: acquaintances would mind briefly,
A few small muddles would be instigated
For somebody else to sort out, the man from the Ministry.
Insurance difficulties to resolve
They'd have to wipe the slate clean
And the dirty window that the sun
Seems misty through, like tears
That endless vale. The threadbare rug,
Pattern of design and wear
Familiar after pushing the carpet-sweeper twice a week
And before visitors. Who were not given the worst cracked cup 'Let not'
A last sip of water, like before everything a silly neurotic habit.
Put the bundle of neuroses on the fire's one bar,
And the cat she couldn't afford out
Of her dreams, before going to sleep head down on knees
Too cold to undress and lie down.
Death is a childhood bird, with its head tucked under its wing
Dead to the world.

He dropped the first glass accidentally,
Then stood spellbound, looking on
Fragmented light, as if drunk
On a famous string quartet, for the first time again
The reefs of broken milk bottle made him feel it
Gently, a child obedient to a forbidden voice, feeling
Irresistibly, he fetched another cut whisky glass
Bounced it neatly beside the other heart.
A double measure of broken glass, flickered
Like burning £5 notes, then there was no stopping him
Nothing was sacrosanct
Glass from photographs performing
The same miracle of October light.
Books by a conscientious student gutted
Along their spine. A veil of
Net curtains pulled down guying him.
He tried to pull an old-fashioned leather arm-chair apart failing
Did he temporarily try to smother himself under its seat's cushion
Or the thwarted childhood, he continued
At prep school, he pleaded to himself
Smashing up someone's property.

THE LADY IS A TRAMP

A sunlit June morning she turned into
The quiet mews; sitting down on the first scrubbed doorstep,
Stick splayed out, half-open parcels all round, battered
Handbag, a Marks & Spencer plastic carrier bag
And a psychedelic one.

Two neat children from next door came out –
They seldom played in the street.
Soon she was yelling at them. Perhaps they giggled,
She waved her stick. Their elderly father came reasoned went
Shepherding his children home.

The owner of the doorstep came, smart, sympathetic
Woman. She brought her a chair
Subtly upholstered, almost antique.
She brought her tea and sandwiches
And phoned for the ambulance.

The ambulance attendants weren't being had.
They drove away, sent a policeman.
A shirt-sleeved youth he reasoned, with force
Led her off, one arm clutching all her parcels
And she leant on him.

Established with initial drinks, another evening
Smoothly prepared, glides into gear;
Well oiled. The liberal predominant mouth
According to their book, and other views
Represented. Wit and aside have their role.
The well-groomed animals sit up and beg.

Claws in, till they're alone
With those they can talk to. Meanwhile the discussion ranges
Northern Ireland, Timothy's new job,
Marriage, two of the three women involved
With married men. 'But' 'after all'
The animals go in two by two

And the rest are left out in the cold.
Rhodesia. Elizabeth's marriage is also discussed
Cannibalistically. A theory flowers,
Backed up with some personal statement –
Guess-work and memory fill in the rest –
Omit the unreasonable or animal.

Enough drink to loosen the tongue enough.
Even the spectre doesn't puke up the meat
And lies. They all get through their hoops
Until the brandy, when appearances can temporarily
Sag: political personal the odd risqué remark half risked.
The well-trained animals know their cue.

Sheer leg neatly crossed: her tempo
Perfectly under control,
As if she'd measured out her life with tipped Gauloises
With her usual aplomb.
All these visitors an essential background element.
'Shall we discuss art then, yours or someone's?'
The keynote ambivalence, some pretty metallic mask
To be whipped off, for the act to stop, penetrating
Tears of a clown, saw-dust and tinsel
Some dusty ideal: tears after the party.
You can take a white horse anywhere.
The crinolines stowed,
Cans of tomato soup for the slashed wrists to hand
But mostly pretty things: echoing another useless era
Her creation, a portrait of someone
On the way to being sent up. With press cuttings.
A chic coat of many colours trailed
A shadow, crying for attention, the spoilt child
Or orphan. Drinking, to nerve nerves
Or unnerve infinitely wants
The same. Not the American dream.
Or crying for the abandoned dresses
Hung in the ancient green rooms,
And the postures left behind.

In the supermarket, across the pavement from the horse
Parked at the kerb all day with the cart,
An old employee bent under a grey nylon overall
Sits at a *check-out point*, temporarily not in use
Eating cherries out of a white plastic container,
And does he dare to take five
Minutes more? More than half
The way done, thinks
A youth on crutches, not too much pain
Caricaturing a face, going for the tube
Down to the trains. No lift.
A girl buys flowers for her flat.
A girl buys flowers for her mother
In hospital. Tulips 'too red in the first place',
And against the grey only the dandelions
Blowing like memory. From the window the endless grey roofs
If one noticed
                    the horse always stands the same way,
His right hind hoof lifted a few inches from the road.
Always the same hoof lifted as if
Once wounded there, a girl thinks I'd rather die
Than see this animal again
The traffic grinds past all day.
People turn down the quieter side streets.
People bring food for the horse, perhaps too much
Or the wrong kind? The owner watches
Sitting beside the tilted cardboard boxes of flowers
Across the pavement, and sweeps up the shit.
Shovel and box are also kept in the cart.
He keeps the horse groomed, the ridge of white hair down its back
And the tufts on its forelegs are clean.
In winter he brings old coats to cover it,
Trembling and when it rains, he throws a horse-cloth over
It. It stands every day with its right hind hoof lifted a little.
As seasons change the colour of flowers
Flares in the shabby cart against the horse's peat-brown flanks.
Some people pat the horse tentatively,

17

Or stroke its nose. Except to turn its head
To be fed, it never moves,
Never shifts the cart, even when the car parked in front of it
Is driven off, leaving a temporary space.
After nine hours in the dusty air
The horse is slowly driven off.
Sitting up with the reins, the owner appears
Old-fashioned. Tall, grey, almost distinguished
Looking kind. Saturdays a shrill woman helps.
His wife? Screaming the flowers like the gypsies
Who also come with their heather and bandied luck,
Battered prams cluttering the pavement, in front of the supermarket
Near where the horse always stands.

The noise of the traffic crashes all round,
Night time is the only quiet time,
In this shopping street.
A policeman walks his beat with careful strides.
A sheet of dirty newspaper is trodden along the pavement
Open at a photograph of a fluffy blonde, in the arms of another man
And another of an earthquake
A hut half broken in the foreground going back
To oblivion. 'Gerry, Gerry' screams
A young mother with a pram guided by one hand
And her toddler pulling with both hands on her free hand.
'You *can't* stroke the horse', 'You never
You never. You couldn't.' A group of school kids
Crashes down the street, screaming
And eating hot pies or fish-and-chips.
A fat girl trundles along behind them
Alone, eating chips. She looks at the horse, glazed
Then lurching to free her black patent leather boot
From a big Woolworth paper bag
Trodden on by everyone. A shabby middle-aged woman
Ambles up with a carrot the horse swallows. A car hoots piercing all the rest
You long for that note to stop. Smoke drifts back
From the cigarette the longest-lashed girl in the group lit
For her boy-friend. Traces of bright paint remain
On the side of the cart. Until he's sold some
The flower-seller leaves in the cart boxes of tulips,

Daffs and narcissi, parchment petals.
Later a black Maria trundles down
At the same time every day, someone going to cross the street
Watches compulsively the slit windows
For the eyes of men, the rows of eyes
Always going past. At ten to four,
And mildly by the kerb the horse
Still stands. His right hind hoof is lifted as if
To scratch the tarmac.
'Uncle Sam wants you,' yells a young male assistant to a supervisor
Inside the supermarket for the hump-backed old man
In grey. A dirty man with wild eyes
Who sometimes minds a fruit stall outside a pub
While the owner's inside, wandering through the crowd
Drops into the gutter
In any temporary break in the line of parked cars
Looking for usable fag ends?
On the pavement passing the horse
Who stands with his right hind hoof slightly lifted
He looks down between its hooves, doesn't notice
The tufts of white hair on its lower forelegs.
A cripple with steel crutches turns into the supermarket
Somehow managing to manipulate a wire basket as well
As the crowd inside. The noise of
The traffic crashes all round. Night time is the only quiet time
In this street 'the noise in my head never stops'
A woman awry, hands to peroxided hair
Zig-zags down the street with tomorrow's hard luck story.
Without any change a man buys flowers
And more bloody tulips are taken off the cart,
And the horse still stands with his
Cart in the row of parked cars, gleaming in the sun.
Faded garlands on the side of the cart also shine
Mistily. A little girl unwinds a skipping rope
With fluorescent handles. In a temporary space
She begins to skip, but there isn't room
– In the supermarket, a store detective observes someone
Placing a tin in her own basket. The horse wears blinkers,
Hurrying past someone looks for
The bit of brown expressionless eye. Same colour as his hair,

Chestnut with darker streaks
And white patches on back and forelegs.
Two girls stop and the blonde buys daffodils
Like many people, they turn to look back
At the horse. 'Got this week's *Woman*?'
Manure not yet swept from the street steams
Into the dusty air, with the carbon monoxide.
Another mother smacks another toddler
Who wants to stroke the horse.
A policeman walks his beat with careful strides.
'Just get the train in time,' muttered under his breath
Clutching his daffs. 'Time of your life, win the time' her magazine
    beckons her
Home to comfort: hurrying past she looks back at
The horse always there.

ATTEMPT

A pull like various tides to avoid
Decision that second clumsy non-decision
You can't rescind. These tracks compress the mind,
Ropes against the sea.
So many stand on the extreme edge looking down
The three-foot precipice.
War-time home, the underground stifles.
The happy people opposite on the adverts glare sweetly.
Beside him on the platform the real ones have problems
And thrills. Easy as swallowing a pill
Hallucinatory. The steel binds his eyes,
The black white light off the rails.
That way, the path over the hill
Has stopped but it doesn't matter.
The tracks sing along his mind
Grooves, off the record run down.
The siren will win
Against the elsewhere bustle of everyday,
That cutting battle. Early commuters will frown.
No gentle reflection hitting the hay
That way. Ophelia's hair swirls
Nursery Gorgon snakes, steeled: flecked with pink daisies.
The mirage sucks.

EVERLASTING FLOWERS (*Helichrysum*)

For C. B.

For her lighting a dim corner
Of the dim room. Golden,
Like the chink of the two half-crowns that had brought them
Home here in this small back room
Still burning months later, against the muddy wall-paper.
Only a few flowers had been knocked off in the confined bedsit
Denuding the grey stalks angularly.
The rare visitors didn't remark on amber flowers
Preferring to ignore the poor room for someone's sake,
Until this one. Talking nineteen to the dozen
Mrs. MacDonald completed her sentence;
The hazy gold scales fell.
She saw them as dusty objects
To be thrown away. – She saved everything
That might come in useful, every paper bag.
But no occasional gift of waxy tulips would ever bloom brighter
Than their tarnished gold:
Imperial purple, dusky plum,
The faded violet no stronger scent
Than their permanent eunuch status.

Through autumn armoured with a dying fall
Hazel and russet blinded, she
Would have hibernated by the misty gas-fire.
Waking slept, through the routine
Eyes drowsy with past
Mirage a few facts rearranged a knight
Who snipped the silky lullabying chords
Established similar gold chains from star to star
For dancing, at the Palais. Chandeliers twinkle
Interchangeable letters flowing
The cliché everything.
First necessity talking over the dead
Facts, new hands wash in soft lights.
She waits with disenchanted grateful eyes.

Secretary bird on off day, or spinster
Living alone, content to be home daily
For her meal, evening's entertainment,
The same glossy package under her arm.
Before the comfort of her electric fire,
As aperitif, attractive illustration.
She checks the familiar menu: Elizabeth or Jinny
Alone and fed-up, but things
Will modulate her elegant despair,
And there is always something to be said for her
Life-style and clothes, and looks.
Meanwhile fish fingers frizzle, quickly downed.
She turns to the rich dessert,
Stockinged feet toasted by the blaring fire.
Jinny's day has got better in a word,
Unfair coincidence her jazzy grandmother with wand:
The drug will work again for her
Magic despite the crows-feet gathered in the mirror,
The usual let down feeling
The ending cheats too much or, that packet used.

PERFUME

The waiting, the worry oscillating
On a chart they might keep of.
Another appointment kept punctually, even early

The waiting: for something to do, at home
Tidying the cheap phials and dusty bottles.
A 'medium range' holder for solid fragrance
In decay more heady
Atmosphere of that past, possessed
Again turning to feel briefly
Down the long avenues of almond blossom,
Students, high on drink and not the settled despair:
St. Agnes' Road. What's in a name?
All that desire and worry, in the spring of it all
Whatever. Put it back to feel
The thrill of total regret another year if?
Temporarily my own madeleine cake, wafer thin.

She envied the way she'd trot straight to him
In any company, sure of a welcome
Whenever she chose to transform herself from a pile of black wool
To a dainty high-stepping missie with wicked eyes
Liquid stabs at her heart, off days.
Though his attitude betrayed little.
The heaped black wool on his office carpet
Perhaps put some visitors at ease,
He walked her in the Park early and late,
At his heels in his smart local;
An undemanding bitch, trotting sedately through
Mr. Scane's working week and appropriate country weekends
And invasions of his mistress,
When she gave her an uncanny feeling
If she caught her eye, she felt she was watched
Not that the decorous bitch showed
Symptoms of possessiveness, sure of her position.
And she couldn't bear the idea of a pet.

YOUNG MARRIAGE

After work, heavy-footed up the stairs
She hears more tremulously now.
Food and telly, telly and sleep half-heartedly
Desired. Some nights are better than others on the telly.
Bottled beer at home, helping to insulate;
Too tired to go to the pub these days.
Perhaps she tried to penetrate the general carelessness
The permanently glazed eyes, like the coat of a sickening dog.
At first he was disappointed falling asleep
In a favourite programme, or a play's story.
Then accepting, grateful to be lulled from that escapism
To a stronger drug. Then he'd stay there
In the chair, splayed like a doll dropped by a giant child
Till he woke in the small hours heaving himself to bed.
The electric fire, so close, that helped him sleep awoke him burnt,
While the meter ticked on, with tomorrow's alarm.
Sometimes she'd thought when his features relaxed
To doziness, that the best moment
But she knew better than to rouse him from the chair.
Going out had become a thing of the past
She joked to her friends, young wives
Mothers about staid middle age
But alone was scared at the thought of
A life of evenings so; then resentful.

UNDERSTANDING GEORGE

Now that she has lost it all
She wants to give him beautiful objects,
Even costly to show how much
She cared.

She understands James now.
Whenever she paid her duty visits
Sandwiched between other appointments in the district,
Whatever she admired in his den of curios
'Would you like it? Take it, my dear,' he'd say
'Take it,' and sometimes eyes soft
'I'd like you to have it.'
Perhaps, the long country evenings
He thought of *his* china poodle on her mantelpiece,
His miniature in her Chelsea flat
Where she only brought him once.

The evening draws in
And we haven't lain in the long grass, daylight
Till ten. This year
The autumn leaves are scars.

She wondered why she still came to see her,
With her impressive collection of people.
But she arrived inevitably on time,
Aura of expensive clothes and life.
She talked of holidays dinners her penthouse husband to whom
En route after her business trip up North:
That devotion lavendered all she said,
Sandwiched in the folds of her white trouser suit,
The top layer in her expanding suitcase.
She'd the edge on her friend just
In the intelligence league-table at school. With the fey
Promise of the rain-crossed window she waits for
Her visit to be over, the phone to ring imagination's shade:
Her voice in different sentences 'Things haven't worked out as.'

MISTRESS

In an interesting corner at parties flared
Wits antennal, arguing better than most men, with them.
Waist-length hair black in shade, cow's eyes
High cheek bones, stooping imperceptibly
Her cigarette clouds her glass
A theory poised, demolishing
Wittily, in a mesh of barbed and desiring looks,
Jagged eyes, remotely drunk,
Never out of control on the social rails anyway.
Dress immaculately untidy, just the dark lady
More extreme than the company, however that varied
Veered bundles of contradiction
'But the new play's purely derivative'
Structural nerves not waving but
Plugged into something electric on the air
During the music and shaded lights.

Ultimately more or less sober, they judge
Or comment on her disappearing to the crouched night
Unless she's picked up someone with her coat,
Wrapped in someone else's heavy cloak
Distantly imparting: auto-electric blanket,
Or taken to bed like a teddy bear to play with.

Onions were hung to ornament the kitchen.
The crash of the sea at the cliffs and time
A gentler element the view, without a storm
The wheeling gulls.

Upstairs poor light, low ceilings.
All the windows rattled. The worn basket chair
That went with the place, background of tenderness
Moss on a stone.

A strip of seaweed flapped by the front door
Though you generally saw the weather blowing up
Out of the windy garden, stories of local drownings;
The mewing gulls.

God the appalling beauty of these places
Visited by dream, or out of time; polluted now.

A keen longing they had for it,
A tracery of fresh weeds in the windy garden.
A mangy cat skulked by the door, let them stroke
Lapped the milk quickly. No trippers' vehicles yet.

Their home a crazy cradle slung
In the wind, and rain insistent at the window
Like the stilled thought. Down by the jetty
Another night the life-boat not put out.

Salt spray sharp in the eyes as they walked by
The sea is the tears his body dries.
Trust, like the tin mined through centuries
Repercussions: the hazy royal myths half cast

Out of fact, glowing. The window creaks;
The walls are paper thin. Tonight they're safe.

SOHO

The names of girls on doors,
Mist of climbing roses over the Square in early summer
The benches filled with loungers, some dirty
Hungry probably. One more couple
Walking through, days of.

The prison wall of *Cinerama*.
Fragrance of foreign food, and petrol
Striptease City a blood-red carnation
In the gutter. Empty spirits' bottles,
The tourists' cars.

The odd car noses its way
Through the crowd almost as thick in the road.
In pretty clothes a fairly rich girl
Holds up a pretty dress against herself,
Against the rattle of small change in the chipped saucer
At the next stall an elderly woman keeps
Prominent among the chipped tea-pots, souvenirs
From sea-side resorts, bric-à-brac so recent
It's faded. The tourists stream past men exhibiting
Monkeys, in bright woollen jackets
Old men's faces people gape at in delight.
A stall of giant candles, as bright as
Their jackets before they burn.
A picture propped against the side of a stall,
A straw-haired pert miss, long cold
Unless imagined, in the road's dust. A nun trips by
Tight conventual purse grasped through the loud tourists
With money to fling about. In and out of the antique shops,
Their cheaper stuff on trestles outside; then the brilliant fruit stalls.
Numbers from the top twenty at different stations
Along the route and dial. The odd policeman.
Behind the vying fruit, Tesco and the other chain stores.
A big polythene bag of old clothes in the road,
Vermilion spilt on asphalt, gold from the mud.
Coveting that cloak, ultramarine, she gave all
Next week's rent. He paid for four dresses for her.
They buy a heap of stuff to sell again cleaned up.
He goes away sad he couldn't buy a picture
For a wall. She buys this dress to dazzle that man.
Tea for the women on the stall and against the cold
Brandy. The inspector winds his way through the market:
It's all done in cash anyway.
A girl with old-fashioned bee-hive hair and drain-pipes
Sits impassively by a rail of fashionable old clothes.
A forties' cotton dress, blue with white spots
With modern tarty make-up, casting an image
Or in her own eyes. An older

Moss green lace creation, in the gutter
Perhaps too tatty to sell: she caresses.
A dressing-gown that could be worn as a light coat:
Someone wore it watching at a sick-bed.
Above, several ten-pound notes are pocketed.
A mongrel sniffs round the polythene bags, is moved on.

KENWOOD

Girls in long skirts, or still almost bare
In the warm evening throng down the paths to the house
With men in beads. Barefoot over the lawn
The couples hand in hand, before the eighteenth century façade.

From beyond the lake at the end of the lawn's vista, hazy music
Night scent closing hot July. Later, moonlight plentiful.
The sylvan symphony was a concert where you paid
To sit on the enclosed grass, and we couldn't stay all night
But it was fairyland.

Now the house is broken open, looted romantically.
'The sedge has withered from the lake.'
The lawns wild. From somewhere sirens wail.
It lives there now in the ruin.

Behind the lofty trees, apparently bosky as ever,
Heaps of refuse, the final powder
The weather does nothing with: that won't break down.
Moonlight still plentiful, not turned off.

Doors splayed like a centipede's legs.
They're off before the train grinds
Still the dusty morning the first scuttle through the ticket barrier
Brief cases bobbing, then the scrum
Commuters siphoned through the platform's bottle neck.
The dim turquoise trains become visible
Lined up beside the smoky morning
Under the cathedral roof. After a pause the cripples,
One or two on each rush-hour train,
Jerk through the early winter morning.
Three puppets more clumsily tweaked
Than the masses: metaphorical trio
With the same sick persistence
Making their way across the larger landscape. A middle-aged man
Leaning heavily on his stick makes steady progress
Leading the handicap home;
An impotent old man more slowly covers the ground successfully;
Finally – polio, a stroke? – a woman's limbs flung wildly on the air,
Crosses the barrier, as the others gain their buses, taxis, offices.

MAN IN THE TEA SHOP

Leant on his elbows on the red plastic table top
Speckled with crumbs,
Through the glass of the hot tea shop,
August afternoon.

A few hours later when I came by again,
Inevitably the same thoughts,
He had only changed his table
And sat staring through the glass
Into the middle distance.

Sometimes her stomach revolts from food,
The ham grey under the strip lighting
However bright outside the supermarket.
The customers are one big mouth
Always open. And their lips, fists tight.
Sometimes summer; the meat goes off before it can be sold
Despite the vast turnover,
They take it off, but some slips through
To be returned by angry customers
Who most likely left it in the sun.
Sometimes she hates the rows of canned food and music
Before going home to open their meal with *Dr Marigold's Prescription.*

In the half-light half-knowing had held
Like her own hair, cut off.
The dial of each rackety week
Slid back to sweet nothing.
In the still street a hackneyed car back-fires.
Time stood still, or waltzed them.
The usual rites of dress and coffee, Mozart at 8 a.m.
Elsewhere, the curtains are drawn.
He winds her up for the week
Or they wound something down.
The worlds of love and sleep dipping,
The week an empty bottle.

GENERATION GAP

Casually against the cemetery railing
Drab green coat buttoned up high, mini-length
A little passé now. Like him. Hair like the current style.
Her transistor held up to her ear.

That put him off straight way. But in any case
Phenomenally he approached her
More pert at close quarters
'What are you listening to?' spliced the tyrannical buzz.

Sounded patronising and was she young!
And chewing gum. 'Luxembourg. Shall I turn it up?'
In the suburban semi-everything between
The intermittent traffic. The homeward rush-hour warmed.

Still perched on the concrete ledge below the railing
Slim legs outstretched, tights *beautifully sheer*.
After a pause that she controlled
'You live round here,' to the paving stones.

Off-hand, mouth curled prettily down.
The tranny continued, a lyric emerged
In the soggy late afternoon, starlings flying
Into London to roost. Traffic reasserted.

Reed voice again, 'I haven't got anything to do,
Till later on,' already played the gamut of diffidence.
Nails colour of dry blood, twilight closing
Quickly in. – Was the car locked?

Her coat the same tone as the evergreens behind
Like a school uniform – as if pursued
By furies of teachers 'I must push on'
Awkwardly into her adult's ingenuous face.

CASE

When she went away to the special home
They'd already missed seeing her around
Zig-zagged zany on the street where
Hair in the wind and eyes
And curiosity and neighbourhood friendliness
Because she was bright and loud.
Freewheeled roller skates or push-bike
Another kid hung on behind
Back from playing round the block, or her Saturday job
Or with the succession of dark youths
Paraded daylight evenings: that summer term,
Magazines stuck out under her arm, pointed the way
To the latest style, in a cheap enough edition.
And the darkest of all most in attendance, dancing
On his motor-bike. They didn't see him bring her back
From the lights and fountains up town
High and soda, she coasted through
She skidded six months ago on the street where
Months now not a magazine's new number.

HANG-OVER

Used to hiding like a sick animal
This time kindness made faint.
The next day he felt better probably
But stayed in bed, lying half in and out
A baby half-way, world-ward
Drifting in and out of
Sleep the rubbish going down a river, in and out of reeds
In dream, flowing down to Camelot.
Head-ache iridescent patches of oil
Polluting the river. Radio,
Irrelevant megaphone from another shore.

STREET FIGHT

Over half the stream of shoppers down the sunlit street
Flashes surprise accusing
In the confined space two youths go for each other
Not sure they saw, blows mostly rained on the air
Creating space for their capered brawl
People push against the line of wire trolleys
And the supermarket's glittering window, or hurry on.
Or step into the gutter as if to avoid getting hurt
Accidentally, or to have passed by
Just not on the ground, neither of them
Yet, gauzy patchwork, splashes like eyes
Half-recognised between giving
And like now twist athletic avoiding hurt
Pride, now people stand and watch
Exhibitionism. Someone considers intervention.
One of them lunges turns marches off
The other reels skips to overtake him,
They go on arguing sullenly
Joint target for the bright eyes of housewives.

No loss in bad reception, knowing
Something almost as nice will succeed,
Like a favourite biscuit;
But sometimes comforting from sheer
Familiarity, off days. And psychedelic modulations.
Or soft tremors in the soft flesh.
Ironing, the hands move a little slicker,
Not wanting this barrage of sound over.
Something almost as nice will succeed.
Sometimes an event tied on as a tag,
Like in a soft film. His arrival,
Swearing, water going down the sink
Changing the record or the news or D.J.
Interrupt the melody all day, night, always to hand.

THE LOST DOMAINE

The flower beds overgrown,
An old bike rusted against the wall
Though it seems every day was fine.
Can't we return to that back yard?
Days of – moss between the crazy paving,
Morning sun; so derelict and safe,
Like children playing behind the ancient gate.

THEFT

The wind sought out vulnerable places
But the sky blue and summer clouds snowballed.
Bare trees in the square told
The season, with her shabby but warmest coat.
That day she was in a good mood, luck on her
Side of the street the sun showered.

Preoccupied about finding the small amount in small change
Without asking the man to change the fiver
She noticed it missing in the fish-monger's.
Gone from her purse where it had glowed
Among the scales of coppers, comforting slither of blue
A promise of fine weather on holiday.

Putting the kippers away blindly she rummaged in her bag
Feeling it wasn't, but believed seeking could find,
Poor enough to be like the woman in the gospel.
Knocked out of her previous high spirits as if
The finger of a god the finger of suspicion
At a stroke, diminishing.

She remembered the small queue in the dairy,
Self-service without enough space by the single cashier,
Wire baskets sticking in people, fingers stuck in.
She'd go back to enquire, but it would be too late,
They wouldn't have time to be sympathetic,
She would be in the way, or telling a story.

The loss shocked her, even chill down the spine
Beyond the pleasure of anything she could have bought,
Though objects paraded tempting towards
Even a coat: it would have vanished
Daily into small economies, redoubled now.
Already she resolved to outdo fate, who cheated her.

Along the street finger-tips met overhead as a bridal arch
Whose stinging flowers she hastened through.

48

The jungle sunshine menaced.
She walked at risk. And no miraculous recovery.
Back to her home's privacy to turn out her bag properly
Feeling it wasn't, but poor enough for a bit of luck.

PORTRAIT

Against the beautiful sets
She's constructed over years, her life tells its story
According to plan. At four o'clock, China tea
From petal thin cups. Church now the hippies' incense pervades
Rehearsed years. Lying about like coffee table books
Her current work: *art nouveau.*
Deliberation, clung moss over everything
With which an image is organised.
People phone and arrive at the arranged times.
A book is published and another nursed.
In clothes from the current cult era
She darts about for additional objects for the pretty picture
She's poised against, butterfly. Bank statements basic
Tucked behind letters from better known acquaintances
Keeping her private gaudy
Precarious craft afloat. Quite a good critic:
Vain. The photographs contrive a demure small girl.
She could still get away with getting
Older, despite the lotions and cauchemar.

We broke a peach's heart to make your hair silkier.
Nobody understands a girl like we do. We've never met a girl
Who didn't want to feel prettier. But do you feel
As good as you feel? Do a good thing to your skin, baby. Fantasy,
The first warm fragrance for the cool generation. Knowing
Is a woman's natural privilege. Feel free. If he likes you now
He'll love you as a blonde. Cheesecake.
Cheese is good for a body. You just feel
Confidently cool. The softest way to natural beauty Sheer Genius
Moisturising make-up. When you mean it wear Affair.
There's one sherry that won't founder on the rocks.
The world's most precious diamond, your own. Why one
Outrageously expensive Emba mink will make you
Reasonably happy for the rest of your life.

Straggling across his same skyline
Skeletal on high blue, losing
To rain and grey. So many drunken figures
Staggered down a hillside, reflections
In a grey crystal. The weather always clear,
Sky white, a bath of grey.
Thoughts had clustered along their branches
Flowered to action time clouds scudding
Or placid, dangerously in the shadow of
Those leaning triffids. Grey over white.
Bits of summer hung on them;
Wool along the hedgerow,
Someone strolling in reverie. They rose
Conning towers. More real than the chimneys, bore down
Or sinuously into waving fronds
Suggested death by water; gazing across from the aquarium
Of that high room. Or transfixed to his ghost
Along a moment's high wire where
Often gazing wistfully to grey
Watched the light, looked up from bed,
Thought a cluster of June notes the siren didn't splice.
Their angles caught the petalled mood,
Pinned for him with their untidy fittings
Taste of time past, grey over white.
These gibbets where a whole existence hung
Still in the balance, seesawed.

Out of the burnt July street, to the new and familiar ambiance
His kind and cruel, shaded off
So many garish flowers. 'He doesn't need to gild the lily.'
In the limelight enough to be criticised.
Several people had already spoken to him
As his bag stuffed with the weeklies dumped somewhere.
For the moment the pictures spoke more convincingly
Remarkably versatile, another of his aspects
Remarkably consistent achievement of cliché disorganized days.
Likenesses nod on the walls, like a careful gardener's
Prize blooms, manured with alcohol and passing
Light affairs so-called. Poor Eve
In the background somewhere as usual
Greyly, like her desiccated painting.
Airily, he'd sipped half, enjoyed the heady bouquet when
She caught his eye, something in the way
She walks to the next picture, stepping over
Three years, with the fetching twenties' bob that
Couldn't replace her endless hair, hymned once.
She noticed him and stared, returned
Punctiliously to the picture she rehearsed,
That cool care almost decided him the pictures withered
Chinese water-flowers Cook bubbling aimed for
Through the faint aware Julian
Curiously staring through the melodramatic black
Magic lantern show, now only grotesques
Postulated the twisted conversation again, down the passage
To the water over this unidentifiable egg-head's shoulder.
A few visibly out of their depth, coming up for air
But mostly beautiful people with it all
From the centre pinion the canvases
With cliché and wit. An older painter who never would make
Anything studied with careful detachment
Opposite to the Jagger one, not sat for, an earlier young man
Outfaced his aging friends.
With the licence of success or sex: they stare
Caught in historic streets under the penthouse

53

From faded *plages*, present background.
Looking at Macmillan, newspaper montage, how
This would have driven the talk then, and the usual
Troupe of posture. Some of Kenneth's originals already dead
And others gazing backwards through the looking-glass
Wistfully over more privately pastoral months
Past selves. The grand conductor not yet ga-ga.
Chance works with diamond artistry, Kenneth
Sticking pins in a canvas to position things
Coincidentally deflated half his sitters:
'All his women have waxy faces.' Her short hair floored him
A self of whose hymned,
The early Kenneth portrait, cleft
By national service. Evelyn biting her nails.
Perspectives jostle, with a conversational hum.
Private lives in the limelight.
From the bottom of a fish-tank a face stares up
Alive and well and living in
Hell. Through the miraging water 'basically derivative'
He got new insight for work in progress. A gap
In the general conversation. Kenneth was on the fringe
With some bird. Figures group in the show
Round the different models of his T.V. set, pulling
The punches for some, or nursery rabbits conjured.
Nerves fully stretched temporarily to pick up the old sensations.
'They're planting plastic trees in Los Angeles.
When you're driving along at 50 m.p.h., who cares?'
Crucified the accent. Kenneth looked tired, considering sales.
The fragile triangles lapse and reform
Differently shaded. Similar vermilion and turquoise.
Not in the limelight enough to be criticised.
Or decoratively with his heart on his sleeve.
'When I saw Kenneth last he was worried about the earlier.'
She worried her image wasn't more attractive
Pretending to look at the picture, she watched
Their reactions snipe. 'But basically,
He's only decorative, in a very austere way.
That's his formula.' Sue nimboed
With lavendered atmosphere he resented.
The trailing design on that shirt

Suggested death by water. 'Diamonds are for ever.'
Years of night didn't even add up to that and galloping
'Inflation' one of the sitters castigated
The present government. Two painter spinsters,
Their middle-aged togs bizarre enough to label them
In their eyes discuss the new gallery charges. Snow
On blue. All responses thrown now.
So the bird women and attendant males gyrate.
If he looked at a zanier gimmick
Seven ideas sparkled, before grey
Wall reasserted itself. Daring to obliterate so much of that face
With a bowl of flowers: the painted face tugged
His gaze swivelled guiltily, chatting to Julian
Why wasn't she still out of his life
Like the floor past rose and Julian
Looked curiously on, commented on a series of self-portraits
Dimmer all the time finally flared
With inane clarity, an illustration for a woman's magazine story,
A progressive one, with a sad ending.
He said, 'Sue's here.' 'Derivative basically,'
And Julian's curiosity veered: 'I like that,'
Defiantly of blowsy anonymous Mrs. Smythe.
'Facile,' said Julian. He discovered his glass refilled and someone
Discussing the Academy's *Art Nouveau* with him,
While Julian groped in the narrated dusty past to slot in Sue
While she moved demurely through his early evening
Attentive to each moment caught, unlike her own old art
While his butterfly gaze confused
Them in a swirl of pastel and said something about it.
He hated her persistent calm like before,
Turned carefully to the picture in hand
And Julian's friend's criticism.

DRUNKS

11 o'clock, and quite a fine night,
No autumn chill.
Beside a boarded-up shop-window, plastered with posters
For pop concerts, the Common Market, and Welsh pony-trekking
Holidays; two of them slumped on orange boxes.
The third is stared at by brisk passers-by,
Flowing white hair accentuates his tan,
Gestures prophetically with a *British Wine* bottle.
Seems he has only trousers and a coat, whose
Deep collar frames nudity.
Town leaves and litter blow along the gutter.
What will they do,
When the light splashing over the pavement
From the off-licence on their right goes out.

EXPERIMENTAL THEATRE

Stiller when the naked girl glides on
Under the cruel acid light.
Or was it only his breath caught
'Promises, promises.' A crowd on tape.
A sheet of pop inundated young men
Elsewhere, shooting through   somebody's mind
As she collided with the stage, what
Childhood games. No milk at home.
They've brought the audience to their feet
Wandering in the dark, previous actors
And all. Newspaper cuttings about Prague are stuck on one wall.
In the pitch black, several cigarette ends
Voices all pitches places giving way
To their owners who weave
More replaced figures. Yesterday afternoon.
Mixture of the self-conscious and enjoyable touching
The idea: earlier sessions emerge in his mind.
Some range freely through the silence or half-thought
That black defines. A theory flowers.
The contours of the room are so familiar to the group.
'Let's get out of here,' scuffling; a pair
Who arrived together. Two hug the wall
Peck at communication 'Brecht, Brecht.'
Memory, memory dressing up as a furry animal
Gloved paws, his clenched fists beating on the dark.
But the total experience
For A alone, than B with C
While D was going afterwards to fuck Lise in Chelsea. The
Waves of sound surround. 'The waves drummed on the shore,
Like turbaned warriors.' Nothing seemed to brush him
Sat in his corner, the sound affecting him. He wondered if
That girl was somewhere in the dark, in shapeless jeans and jersey
Bra-less, despite the earlier clinical
For him – like dance only better communication
Dressed in the artificial dark, true mummers
'They'll stone you,' 'They'll stay with us,'
Time for the lights to go on. 'Time ladies, please.'
The pin-striped gent who strayed obscurely in, strays off.

That song, that academic afternoon, that pretty aura
So gone. Tone that the setting made
Sentimental floated across the lawns
And mannered social occasions. Love linked
                              arms burst through,
The uniformed line caves ridiculously in.
Cohorts of shouts criss-cross.
A young constable's especially peaked face.
His ringlets; her ordinariness if she's with him.
Anger across most faces. A strong slogan
Marches across the racket. Boots
And arms
          across the carpet
Where they contort, the record repeats
Some phoney atmosphere blows up
Rocks them deeper
Mutual whatever. That's my regret.
Oh the quick flower and
Rhythm everywhere. Feeling relaxed,
Feeling good stoned mad to repeat
Did they find that
Along the primrose path to the gold at the bottom
Of the nerve-bow. Red face
Frog eyes bulging anger, helmet aimed for
They beat them back. A banner torn.
A girl dragged off, blonde in the dust
Noticed more than this man badly hurt
For ever walking wounded, mentally, after this October afternoon.
Two on to one everywhere. This fight more real than Vietnam now.

MARY PICKFORD

Large dogs abound; pastel dresses
With long sashes, strolling through pleasant gardens
To *happy days*. No black, flicker of grey, only the time
From before they met. Despite some realistic movies,
How safe that world seems; apparently bomb,
Hitler free. Watching, one or two old enough to remember
Those days: girls whose clothes
Portray the cult era.
He watches her sash bounce gently on her arse
As outside he watched her twenties' cap, for some
Pretty ways, and for some badge
Against something now. A few technical connoisseurs,
And for the entertainment, the usual lure of dipped lights
The usual democratic audience.

No regrets past that anyway.
Slate eyes sky she lies and waits
For one of her new friends to fetch up here
Only not the one who was here last night
The other side of the last drink
Sipping night to this gay and brash accompaniment.
Why didn't she struggle up somewhere
Smash the record instead of repeating infinitely
Through the grey white light of gaping afternoon
Suspended between spring and autumn,
Eighteen and past it. Metalled voice, the gentle lining
The lie, walk down the street and no one
And it doesn't matter only the growing yearn, like that before
Lie on, till they come greyly round and try and suggest
Something, or they bring more.
One big hang-up dug in
Eating the motley and semi-criminal past.
And surreptitious chain-smoker years ago, the sex game over
Like the fag-end of Aldermaston, fiddling with the syringe for the next
Experience *la vie en rose*. No one sees
Out in the snow, the clichéd sparrow hopping on the sill.

ADVANCED CASE

I must pick this up do it:
Some release that way the vacuum across the carpet
At right angles to the predominant pattern.
Only the thought cavorts.
Too nervous to breathe
One day I shall die so dizzily paralysed
Among all the undone housework
Left high and dry from lack of confidence not inclination.
Fearing to sweep the floor
Badly fearing to be the figure who is
Sweeping the floor fearing
Contortions of purple, who sweeps a room as for
His sake, head down on knees, sitting fears
To tackle it all undone
Because it has waited so long, mounting
Fear to change the course of events, that flickered is:
The pattern of dust on the furniture
Under which she drowns. Soon she will fear to eat
To disturb the decaying food.
She fears the action that will relieve
Her head fearing she won't do it properly
Her head a postulated mother scolding her
Into her grave. When he comes home
And she spreads her day's tiny achievement thinly
Across the years.

ROAD ACCIDENT

John, walking up the High Street thoughts away,
Mind nearly slipped off the page,
Nearly stepped off the kerb.
One of those people always in a hurry
He'd often step into the gutter, not always looking behind
But then, he followed the pram and gaggle of small kids
As the motor bike roared by, another long-haired youth on the pillion
Cutting up between the kerb and the almost stationary line of cars.
Then he felt he walked the high wire.
All plans frustrated, if survived
The mind impaired, flapping like an open door
Letting it all in. Christ.
A quiet afternoon, and fate's zany chain
That nearly made all afternoons the same.
As the older generation says 'before the war,'
He would say 'before my accident,' if
He said. The arterial gossamer.
Just alert enough for the motor bike's faint burr,
Like a nurse rustling down the ward.

JETSAM

At a bird's-eye view it would be a large field
Ringed with horse-chestnut trees,
And a large red brick house at one end.
For him, the grass at his feet;
Daisies already growing over them or nothing
Green and blue. Not registering vacantly
A cabbage butterfly.

Children spring and are withdrawn
As I before my earlier years
Where now parade the voluntary people.
Nearer the gap in a garden
Than anywhere else in the room,
In an English sexual freedom.

Chapped hands lie useless through summer,
Dotted with blood like poppies scattered
Over the desolated fields.
A hand-washing obsession, like the ambitious.

They say no trouble, clean
Dressing itself, simply
Not interested. They don't say but various I's see
What dem pearly eyes do see?
Registering vacantly a cabbage butterfly.
Like the cash-register she dully rang up
All day, his old mate hadn't liked that dolly bird
(All dirty, flashes of white
Dazzling, grateful obscurity returns.
No green days, blue days; all at sea.)
Is that what knocked you down finally?
After years of back-breaking work
This more aching redundancy, unimproved slum,
When that empty puss you late made wife
Finally flounced out, with the plumber?

FLOOR

Soon it will wall in.
A prison of rectangular blocks;
Each with fine lining of dust
Sanded, colour dust of autumn leaves
Imperceptibly changes, where people have walked more or less
To cross a room and their destiny.
Larger specks of dust for stars; September sky ebbed
Colour of dirty parchment, old skin
Like mind or days trodden on.
For amusement a clockwork mouse of vision
Off course all over the cell the grid structures
A maze of little cracks, wrinkles
Or the nape's deeper network, over a block
Wearing the patina of blue days and skin.

How it spun
Fantasy desert mirage where new animals trek
Mirror stability, the familiar lands
With the occasional money-spider for luck.
Sand in the eyes, a grain in the way.
Below the boards, rifts of ore
Where nightmare's pent, varied cast,
Behind the forehead, without any illusion of
Substantiality the floor runs down
To the waters of the moon:
Their eyes glazed with snow, not wanting
To continue to crawl like a fly or toddler
Painstakingly manoeuvring, time out of mind,
Whatever obstacles in the way of.

Repeated like a musical phrase
The drowsy rhythm of the grid, deserted town
Or lover's star-crossed palm. A ghost like sunlight
Fast in Pompeii, mazy with latter-day thought.
Private pyramids of chance and query
Sink in the blind sandstorm staring into

The floor's wall. With effect
A shadow intersects, would tell the faded hour.
A cigarette packet dropped, a localised bomb.
Each line a minute in the face of
All the rest mirrored, for beady eyes.
Apparently cracked tracery twins the hardening arteries
Soon to be laid there when the floor's
Eaten everything, bland in the sun.

'All art,' he said, 'is exhibitionist,
A man behind a tree showing off his prick,'
As they lay supine by the gyrating fire
The quick flower crumpled to ashy gilded monuments,
She was busy crying for the hopelessness of it all.

Volkswagen Cinzano the Bianco rainbow Piccadilly, over the crowd
Drop-outs, in talk, *the large work largely done.*
Heath meets Mujib. Necessary to measure out much happiness
To wipe away the hurt dog look in eyes,
Even if there wasn't much there before.

DREAM

Doors splayed caves waiting people;
Things were happening as he'd foreseen. *Than gin-&-limes*
Cooler his travelling bag of decision in hand
Shell of quiet, the passer-by on the other side
Himself mingling in the crowd, around the disturbance
Later news-reel of soldiers and personal
Through the green hills of day-dream the dream blasted.

Actual as he'd imagined it the train a stage toward away.
Walking across the platform he pulled himself up sheer face
Climbing on ropes of golden chord the intercom supply lines cleared.
High on cheating and true memory some inner logic
Conducted him along the high wire career's hot line
Electrocuting the familiar shadow, the differently shaded map:
Outside hot sun white wall blue sky of night.
What was she doing here, couldn't get time off that time of day
Despite other people in front at the barrier the same sensation
Puzzle and moon glow. Oranges and lemons. Everything like for real.

At the back of the house, fading sun
Turns to small gold change leaves of the tree,
The table dappled to a chess-board like fate
With the shadow a hazy figure. Temporarily
Out of earshot, kids play on the street where
A rusty bike has been abandoned. A Pakistani youth
Rides a few yards. Soft ideals like love and a cottage
Blossom in the early autumn evening, in Harringay.
From next door Radio Luxembourg mixes with the sensation
A cocktail: through the smoky glass
Beyond the mythical peninsulas of day-dream, some warmth
To plug into at work in the market.
Time has a different texture despite
The news Ulster redundancy, heightened perceptions.

DRUNKS

Her eyes narrowed she talks non-stop
The usual effect of penumbra along the opposite roofs,
Worries images lovers money intimate worries
Rabelaisian and gracious pageant. The other laid aside
Her glass to dream, remorse in counterpoint.
She watches her, veered towards the sordid
Hotel room, no more cheques
Most friends departed, the procession into morality
Plays the familiar year on wretched year.
She smiles over Eve, I lost the thread
Among references to other people, roles
That show success near misses. Glasses and bottle
Washed up on the shore of her babble:
Closeted into middle age, evening has buried them.

THE LITTLE PEOPLE

Fingers root through the work basket
Tug at the darning wool then a red thread,
Busy kitten unwinds a reel,
Jangle this thin green line of thought.
The little figures scurry out into twilight
After they've been packed away in the toy-box
Or the out-tray, at the bottom of the garden:
A school playground of screaming kids
Or a haunting like love. Bureaucracy of nerve.
Cheeping a gothic fantasy erected
Eighteenth century bird-cage head gear for a lady.
A city crowns him, domestically
At risk. Any soft pillow to lie on:
They crawl out bugs, the figures come to do their number.

BLACK ROAD SWEEPER

Out at wintry first light, guiding his mechanised cart
His shovel's clack notches the stucco fronts.
As well as sweeping the gutter he collects
The psychedelic carriers of refuse daily sprouting
By dustbins permanently left out. Attractive youth black power
Sweeping the streets the quiet early mornings
Spring birds sing in the square
No missing coconut trees for the second generation
However pea-souping the fog. He could pick up gossip
About the residents, noticing
The odd person who doesn't live there leave early.
One girl regularly, tell-tale clatter of heels,
Neither notices either, he goes to work later
When he's doing another street. A cat
Well-fed but always on the streets
Flows under a parked Jaguar.
Bizarre council worker, out early on Sundays
Spectral even Boxing Day, or had the spinster
Who saw all he missed dreamt that
With the phobias not calmed successfully by a Monday Club father
Of the little boy capering there under a mock policeman's helmet.
The same kind of rubbish collects at the same places
Every other day, spirits' bottles, newspapers
And the paper chase from correspondence destroyed
By the local Women's Lib. leading light
Though the watcher at the window hasn't pinned that on her yet.

DREAM

She's the girl in the picture again, time
Rescinded. Her own perfume
Not worn since mixes with the cigarette
Burnt out in the ash-tray
To the astringent cocktail of past.
Tights *beautifully sheer, confidently cool*
The door-bell rings, fire-engines to her faint.

Tonight she doesn't hear the dying cry
Or hears them less impatiently.
Mozart's complete.
The women's magazine story is amusing
Not the ultimate in aspiration.
The path over the next hill continues,
Without bomb craters by the wayside
The flowers of the field, and no poppies
For remembrance. The garden recurs
And they wander: till the watchman's hour.

Storms and winter receded
It would be good to go out now,
Brief candle fluttering in the old twilight,
This tangy dust. Perhaps the animals know.

Wrapped in affection's heavy mantle
Night clung about the cottage, distances drowned,
The embers glow comforting
Like memory, not sharp from not mattering:

The hunger will be staunched
Again. Chair and table not scary now.
Occasional glory of a leaping flame
The quick flower, highlights used dishes, the papers.

The room home again, pleasant to fall asleep,
Like the village kids' dog at the vet.

Her maroon nail against the empty glass
Tapping as previously a fan. 'The salary wasn't adequate.'
'Julian's in Edinburgh now.' 'I can't
Think why.' 'He's advising –'
Neat blue suede shoe trims the leg,
His appraisal also taken in by other eyes
And lights a cigarette. 'Beth's not married now?'
'On *fairly* high authority.' 'And with the Common Market.'
Ash fallen like the tawdry snow last night, driving
Against the pane, their shared view.
'Beth married? When?' 'Oh anything, white.'
Her shoe cups . . . and jaded through
The social hours to lie alone.
With pretty pills and fantasies. Off fixing drinks
With the waiter. 'Timothy tomorrow.' 'Yeah
A director now.' 'The youngest ever.'
He picked a rose from the glass bowl,
Not as good as the table,
And gave it to her, embarrassed for their host
Clutching it lankly, dripped down her regulation
Little black dress, as she damned it. 'But the cast
Were weak. The sets a little bizarre.'
'He was superb,' drinking like breath, not
Many noticed, taking the opportunity to talk to Guy.
(Figures off the cuff, always a stumbling block.)
'Tomorrow, with luck; I'll call you at the office.'
'The constituency party won't like it.'
'Going on to Guy's place,' across the room:
'Call a taxi, love.' Jazz subtly turns
The blood. 'And with the Common Market.'
So the bird women and attendant males gyrate
With the licence of success or sex.

Now she was ready, in an aura of moth-balls.
The turning-out had been finished, almost.
The oldest batch of receipts
Meticulously kept for seven years, had been destroyed.
Few for each year, and getting fewer.
Sparse personal letters held together by a rubber band.
A pack of playing cards whose forties' box
Had finally collapsed rehoused in an economy size match box.
And the spare Book of Common Prayer re-covered.
Each drawer lined with fresh newspaper.
Their contents so slight they rattled when opened
Except the clothes' drawers, though almost as bare,
With pale satin bags of lavender.
Nothing out of place; not much
To tidy this time. The annual shrinking bundle
For the Oxfam shop is neatly tied.
Not many clues as to identity for next of kin.
Only the clichéd yellow photo
Tucked in an envelope, a young officer's peaked face
And a rarely subjective sigh
Seeping through the two rooms the sea through a wreck
What a terrible Martha.

PIGEON

Near where the street widens to another set of traffic lights,
A pigeon pecks about the pavement:
Outside a small Indian restaurant, perfume
Drifts down the empty terrace opposite
Waiting for renovation, demolition.
Whenever somebody almost treads on it loud flutter of wings
Flaps a few inches scarcely rising from the pavement.
It drinks from a puddle in the road.
Slate sky buildings colour of their feathers.
A film on some of the puddles in the rainlit street
In this twilight area, brilliant traces of oil,
Similar vermili on and turquoise
Lurk in the pigeon's plumage, and brightly ringing its neck.